DEMAND FOR PAKISTAN

RELIGIOUS AND SECULAR POLITICAL PERSPECTIVES

QURATULAIN FATIMA

CONTENTS

Many authors have delved into the Ideology of Pakistan and have come up with one or the other explanation. In analyzing the authors like Christophe Jaffrelot who characterized Pakistan as "nationalism without a nation"[1], Farzana Shaikh has argued that it is this identity crisis that lies at the roots of Pakistan ; that Pakistan was insufficiently imagined reflects the existing consensus in Partition historiography that this nation-state emerged in the context of a sharp disjuncture between inchoate aspirations of Indian Muslim masses and secret politics of their pragmatic but ambivalent political elites who were primarily responsible for its creation.[2] Author narrates that the most powerful argument in this regard has been made by the historian Ayesha Jalal who began her seminal work with the question, how did a Pakistan come about which fitted the interests of most Muslims so poorly? In addressing this puzzle, Jalal analyzed the movement for Pakistan through the Muslim League leader M.A Jinnah' s angle of vision , primarily taking into account the actions and imagined political strategy of this "sole spokesman" of the Indian Muslims. In a novel and controversial thesis which has become the new orthodoxy in the field, she argued that a separate sovereign Pakistan was not Jinnah's real demand, but a bargaining counter to acquire for the Muslims, political equality with the numerically preponderant Hindus in an undivided post-colonial India. On the other hand, The historian Anita Inder Singh in her spirited response from Oxford demonstrated in great detail how

---

[1] Dhulipala, V, "A Nation State Insufficiently Imagined? Debating Pakistan in Late Colonial North India" (Indian Economic Social History Review, 2011): 377-405.

[2] Ayesha Jalal, *The sole spokesman: Jinnah, the Muslim League, and the demand for Pakistan* (Cambridge University Press, 1985), 1-310.

Jinnah clearly envisioned Pakistan as a separate sovereign state and out-maneuvered a war weary British establishment and the India National Congress led by "tired old men" as Nehru put it, to successfully accomplish his goal. Yet, while refuting the Jalal thesis, Singh agreed with her that Pakistan was a vague concept and that it meant all things to all Muslims.[3]

The Author, however, tests the hypothesis that the support and rejection of Idea of Pakistan was a an ideology supported and refuted on the basis of each and every Political Party's communal Interests.

II POLITICAL SCENARIO PRIOR TO DEMAND FOR INDIAN SELF DETERMINATION

The process of re organizing the Indian society by the British Raj into the Castes and creeds of the British raj started a process of collaboration with the local people as materialized through the electoral system. This election system required the creation of political parties within the frame work of the modalities of British raj. The initial setup of Indian national Congress was encouraged by the British Rulers so as to engage the elite in administration of the Indian Sub Continent.

---

[3] Anita Inder Singh, *The origins of the partition of India, 1936-1947* (Oxford University Press, 1987), 45-230.

The creation of parties like Indian National Congress (1885), All India Muslim League (1906), were initially created to create loyalty among the rapidly English educating Native Indian Elite on the behest of the Ruling British.

Indian politics were an interconnected system working at different levels; and government had much to do with the linking of these levels. Imperialism built a system which interlocked its rule in locality, province and nation; nationalism emerged as a matching structure of politics. The first moving engine in the emergence of the modern political nation was British imperialism. The British imposed an administrative and political matrix in which the Indian nationalist organization.[4]

The Muslims had initially remained distanced from the British Raj, nursing a genuine grudge against them for having established their colonial rule by deposing the dying Muslim Imperial Rule in India. While those hostile feelings led to the isolation of Muslims , their rejection of the Western education stunted the growth of their middle class and business class. The Muslim reformer and educationist, Sir Syed Ahmed khan had supported the British during the 1857 Independence movement but , at the same time, realizing the backwardness of the Muslims pleaded they should go for the modern education and remain loyal to the Raj. By this time the Muslim elite had realized that they were being left out behind in almost all spheres of life by the Hindu majority who were once their subjects.

---

[4] Howard Spodek, "Pluralist Politics in British India: The Cambridge Cluster of Historians of Modern India", Vol. 84, No. 3 (The American Historical Review, 1979): 688-707.

Although the Indian Hindus and Muslims joined hand together during the Khilafat and non- Cooperation movement but this era of Pan-Islamism had finished by the 1930s and the Two nation theory had been adopted by the All India Muslim League.

III BEGINNINGS OF THE TWO NATION THEORY

Three stages in Muslim national evolution were discernible in the century immediately prior to the establishment of Pakistan, and purposeful leadership played a decisive role at each stage. The Indian Muslim renaissance of the nineteenth and early twentieth century was the intellectual formative period of the nation, and was characterized by three main trends : a rapprochement with western science and knowledge , a rediscovery of the principles and the past glory of Islam, and an impetus towards the creation of a new Islamic democracy. The brilliant efforts of the pre-league Muslim leadership in awakening the Muslim pride in aftermath of 1857 were responsible for bringing the fruit of this phase of Indian Muslim development. A Muslim Political organization came into being in Calcutta just one year after the establishment of the Indian association. This was the Central national Muhammad an Association founded by Syed Amir Ali in 1877. As the British government moved ore towards self rule, first through the Minto-Morely reforms resulting into the enactment of the Government of India Act 1919 and then as a result of the Government of India Act, 1935, the Muslim elite s demand to ensure their share in the government on communal basis gathered momentum.[5] They felt that since, in a democratic dispensation it was the numbers that mattered, there was clear indication that the Hindu majority would finally have more power after being ruled by the Muslim Invaders for about six centuries.

The Muslims have asking for a separate electorate as early as 1882, thus sowing the seed of Pakistan without realizing that ultimately it might lead them to seek a separate homeland. [6]

IV   PRO –PAKISTAN POLITICAL PARTIES

a)   All India Muslim League (AIML)

To understand the ideology of Pakistan, it is necessary to articulate the journey of All India Muslim League from its conception to the humungous achievement of Pakistan.The Foundations
The success of the deputation of to Lord Minto in obtaining the assurance of separate electorate created the need of the separate Muslim political Organization to express the communal policy. The guiding spirit behind both the deputation and the resulting permanent political organization was the Sir Syed's immediate successor Mohsin ul Mulk. After preliminary correspondence between Mohsin ul Mulk,Viqar ul Mulk, and the Agha Khan, a meeting of Muslim leaders was hold on 30 December, 1906at Dacca where the Mohammadan Educational Conference was in session and at this meeting the decision was taken to establish the All India Muslim League. [7]

---

[5] S.P Cohen, *The Idea of Pakistan* (Washington D.C.: Brookings Institution Press, 2004), 34.

[6] Ibid, 49-132.

[7] Ibid.

Initial Policy: 1906-1912

The All India Muslim League was founded as a deliberative body-a forum for expounding and exchanging of Muslim political opinions. It was also intended as a political lobby to safeguard the Muslim rights in all spheres of Government. One of the initial defined objectives was to enhance loyalty towards the British Government.

Era of Political Experimentation: 1913-1929

The AIML included the efforts to promote the friendship with other communities especially Hindus during this era and more importantly a demand for self Government in the India. During the Era Muhammad Ali Jinnah was hailed as Ambassador of Hindu Muslim unity. This was the era of the *Khilafat* movement and the Non-Cooperation movement in wake of the occupation of the Ottoman *Khilafat* of Turkey by the Allied Forces during World War I. The era also saw a power struggle among the moderate and extremist factions of the All India Muslim League.

Afterwards , The League itself split , promptly over the issues of separate electorates versus the Joint electorates. Sir Mohammad Shafi s group supporting the separate electorate and Mohammad Ali Jinnah s group supporting the Joint electorate (Dehli Proposals). Mr. Jinnah s group however had to retreat as another "Lukhnow Pact" could not be pulled due to the general Public mood in post *Khilaft*-Non Cooperation Movement. If Jinnah has been able to secure even temporary recognition of his Delhi Proposals from Congress in order to ally Muslim fears, he might have possibly convince a number of Muslim leadership to join Congress for struggle for united Independent India. Had Jinnah won the political control of the Muslim and gone to the subsequent Roundtable conferences with the mandate of the Muslim Community to work for United India , it is at least conceivable that the course of the history in Sub Continent would have been Different.

What in fact, happened that in 1929 was that the potential Bridge between the Muslim Communalists and the forces of greater Indian Nationalism ; namely the Jinnah-nationalist wing of the Muslim League was permanently destroyed. Subsequently the meeting of the All India Muslim Conference was the most representative since the Simla Accord. It was attended by the Delegates of *Khilafat* Movement, *Jamiat - ul-Ulema Hind*, and both the Jinnah and Shafi sections of Muslim League. Jinnah formulated on Behalf of this "united Front" the famous "Fourteen Points" that became the basis of Negotiation between the Muslims and other Parties for Years. The most important points were that the Indian constitution should be federal, with residuary power resting in the provinces; representation at the center should be at least one third of the total, subject to voluntary renunciation; Muslim majorities in Bengal, and the Punjab should be maintained; Sindh and Baluchistan should be separate provinces; and they and the Morth Western Frontier province should be given a measure of autonomy equal to all other provinces; no cabinet, central or provincial shall be formed without one third population of Muslim Ministers, and Muslim religion and culture must be safeguarded through constitutional provisions.[8]

[8] B. R Nanda, *Gandhi: pan-Islamism, imperialism, and nationalism in India* (Bombay: Oxford University Press, 1989), 130-149.

The Critical Years: 1930-1935

The period between the 1930 and 1935 was critical for the Muslim League and for the Muslim community. While the League nursed the wounds of its recent internal civil war, the principle leader involved in that struggle left for London to be part of the Round Table Conference with the British Government.

It is significant that all these Indians whether arch-communalist, prenationalist, pro or anti British, agreed on three fundamental points. First, that the Indian national movement has now aroused the masses to the extent that nothing short of full *Swaraj* was acceptable. Second, that they, as Muslim leaders were willing to conduct peaceful negotiations with Britain designed to establish India as a Dominion but , finally, that they would never agree to any plan for a government of India that did not recognize the Muslim's right to concessions which would preserve their community as a distant political entity.

The communalist speeches of the Muslim leaders present at the Conferences especially that of Muhammad Ali Johar came close to the concept of "Muslim Nationalism". He articulated as

"It is wrong conception of religion you have, if you exclude politics from it. Its not dogma; it is not ritual; religion, to my mind means the interpretation of life. I have a culture, a polity, an outlook on life – a complete synthesis which is Islam;;If you ask me to enter into your Nation or your empire by leaving that synthesis, that polity, that culture, that ethics, I will not do it. My first duty is to my Maker."[9]

---

[9] B. R Nanda, *Gandhi: pan-Islamism, imperialism, and nationalism in Indi*a (Bombay:

The Muslim leaders phrased their demands for Muslim Nationalism in western terms. The subconscious awareness of the terms *dar ul Harb* and *dar ul islam* remained an undertone in the Muslim Leaders speeches.

While the conferences were going on in London, The famous poet, Sir Muhammad Iqbal was asked to preside over the League session in Allahabad in 1930. Iqbal was not a politician, his purpose of speaking was to advise the Muslims the course of action in the current state of Nation. He proposed the idea of a separate homeland for Muslims and doubted if being two distinct entities Muslims and Hindus could live together. His full length of speech however implied that Muslim state was not to exist independently but was to be linked to the all India Federation.

The conferences failed as Muslim Delegation didn't withdraw demand for separate electorate and Gandhi led Congress Delegation refused to step back from joint electorates without reservation of seats. As a result Gandhi presented a scheme which was basically a representation based on Nehru Report. The Muslims, together with the depressed classes, Indian Christians and Anglo Indians, produced a joint statement of demands. Neither side compromised on their demands or seriously contemplated a middle road such as joint electorates with reservation of seats on the population basis, or on any well defined system of proportional representative.

Oxford University Press, 1989), 156.

Quaid e Azam and Rise of Muslim Nationalism: 1937

The elections of 1937 became a definitive point in the Demand for Pakistan in the League's struggle. The defeat of the Muslim League in the 1937 elections in Muslim majority areas led the Muslim League to rely more on the religious slogan to gather the support of Muslim masses. The Muslim masses experienced the rule of Hindus quite closely for the first time and the fear of loss of identity was magnified in the Muslim Minority provinces. This gave impetus to the Muslim masses and middle class support to the earlier elitist Muslim League.

Achievement of Pakistan: 1936-1947

The All India Muslim League at its twenty –seventh annual session, in Lahore, 22-24 March 1940, declared that Muslim India would not be satisfied until the federal scheme of the Government of India Act 1935 was entirely set aside and the whole constitutional plan reconsidered anew, and formally resolved that, in its view,

"No constitutional plan would be workable..or acceptable to the Muslims unless it is designed on the following basic principles, viz, that geographically contiguous units are demarcated into regions which should be so constituted , with such territorial readjustment as may be necessary , that the areas in the North-Western and Eastern zones of India should be grouped together to Constitute Independent states in which the constituent units shall be autonomous and sovereign."[10]

Despite the rather vague wording of the resolution, The Indian press quickly grasped its significance and termed it as the Pakistan Resolution after the terminology used a few years earlier in the writings of Chaudhry Rahmat Ali of Cambridge.[11] The 1946 Election were contested by the AIML on one agenda point that "do Muslims want Pakistan or not?" Interestingly AIML swept the Elections in the Provinces like UP, Bengal, Bihar whereas it did not do well in Punjab.

[10] F. Shaikh, *Making Sense of Pakistan* (London: Hurst & Company, 2009), 116.

[11] Ibid, 124-158.

THE APPEAL OF IDEA OF PAKISTAN

The Idea of Pakistan appealed to all the Muslim Classes of the India. For the middle class aspiring to the government posts , merchants needing government licenses and other services, all those who hope to attain government scholarships , to teach , to practice law, viewed Pakistan as a place where their advancement would not be forestalled by the more advanced Hindu.

The religious fervor of the Indian Muslims as obvious during the Khilafat movement had never accepted the *fatwas* declaring the India as *"Dar ul Harab"* and continued to regard all non- Muslim administration as the apostate. The increased communal pride and actual strength of the Muslim community was the steady growth of the community in India , especially in Bengal , due to high birth rate and continuous conversions. For Muslims in Bengal and elsewhere, therefore, Islam was a vital and ever growing force.

PROPAGANDA FOR PAKISTAN

During 1940, 1941 and 1942 the League publicized Pakistan un-ceasingly. The League's propaganda in this short period was called by one observer " the most significant process in Indian Moslems of recent years"[12] The idea of Pakistan put the Muslim imagination on fire and AIML drew the Indian Muslims to itself like a magnet.

---

[12] MRT, (Urdu Academy Sind for the Toosy Foundation, 1992), 1-212.

Prolific Propaganda appeared in the English and Urdu Press and a rash of books and pamphlets appeared stating the case for the Muslim nation. Muslim teachers taught their pupils the Pakistan creed, and the women 's subcommittee worked to publicize the doctrine among the Muslim women at every social level, both in and out of *pardah*. Pakistan was publicized through the students as well as peasants.

At the time the Muslim League published two books name "Pakistan and Muslim India" and Nationalism in Conflict in India" By a Mr. MRT in support of the idea of Pakistan. The arguments put forward by these books became the basis for the debate for Pakistan in the Urdu and the Indian Press.

The first book, Pakistan and Muslim India", sought to prove on the basis of past history and current example that Pakistan was the only solution to India 's constitutional problems. One section of his book is particularly interesting for it reveals one of the main propaganda lines being used by the league in its campaign in the Frontier province. The crux of the argument was:

"Unfortunately, the Pathans have been duped at present by a false sense of exaltation which their great leader khan Abdul Ghafar Khan enjoys in congress ranks. Mahtama Gandhi is shrewd enough to honour the Frontier Gandhi and consults him on all matters of high policy..Stress laid on non-violence may have been really designed to shatter the Pathan's belief in the non violence and thereby disarm him and minimize his importance as a military factor. There could be no better method of overcoming the possible Frontier danger than by converting a powerful section of the Pathans as camp followers of

Congress, Gandhi had done a great service to the Hindu Community. He has taken the first step in dispelling their historic fears that the Frontier is a danger zone for India". [13]

The second book titled "Nationalism in Conflict in India" cited the comments of prominent Hindus and Muslims on the Two nation theory, argued on the basis of political experience else where that democracy could function only in a reasonably homogenous society, and enumerated the many Hindu-Muslim differences which he implied would make the development of such homogeneity impossible.[14]

[13] F. Shaikh, *Making Sense of Pakistan* (London: Hurst & Company, 2009), 120.

[14] Dhulipala, V, "A Nation State Insufficiently Imagined? Debating Pakistan in Late Colonial North India" (Indian Economic Social History Review, 2011): 377-405.

b) Jamiat Ulema e Hind- Shabbir Ahmed Usmani Group (Jamiat – Ulema –e –Islam)

Maulana Shabbir Ahmed Usmani was one of the few Deobandi Ulema that supported the Pakistan Movement. The Jamiat Ulema e Hind was a staunch enemy of the idea of Pakistan on the stance that there is no concept of a Muslim State with boundaries. However, the Ulema like Maulana Shabbir Ahmed Usmani, Maulana Ashraf Ali, Maulana Zafar Ahmed Usmani and Mufti Muhammad Shafi. This came as a valuable support to the cause of Pakistan. The Jamiat-Ulema-e-Islam was therefore in October, 1945. Jamiat-ul-Ulema Islam became a big landmark in the way towards the achievement of Pakistan. When Mufti Muhammad Shafi joined Jamiat-ul-Ulema Islam , he went all out in support of Pakistan through his pen in favour of Pakistan through his writings. Besides writing he made all out tours of the Sub-continent to motivate muslims in cause of Pakistan. His efforts made their impact mainly on the Muslims of then NWFP (now KPK) referendum in favour of Pakistan. In the election of 1945-46 Muslim League faced a humiliating defeat against the coalition of Khan Brothers and Congress. At that juncture the efforts of Shabbir Ahmed Usmani, Mufti Muhammad Shafi, Pir sahib of Manki s Shareef and Pir Sahib of Zakori Sharif made mobilization of support for Pakistan Possible.

The arguments of Maulana Shabbir Ahmed Usmani were:

- ✓ He first put the Muslim League' s two Nation theory beyond critique by the more veracious Muslim critics   by emphasizing Pakistan to be a reconstruction of the Prophet's Muslim State of Medina.

- ✓ He used the term "Pure Land" and Medina interchangeably to solidify their connection in Muslim minds. This argument countered the more extreme argument of the Jamiat Ulema Hind and the Congress that there is no concept of a Muslim state with territorial Boundaries in Islam. He declared that like medina, Pakistan will be created and flourish with the close Cooperation of "Muhajareen" and "Ansaar".[15] In other words the Pakistan will be created and flourished with cooperation of the Muslims from minority provinces like UP (Muhajirs) and Muslims of provinces constituting Pakistan.(Ansars).

- ✓ He also reiterated that Pakistan will be a state where Ulema have complete contribution in making laws and implementing them. Indeed the JUI 's founding charter declared that it was " against the evils of Gandhism, Communism and Godless Politics of Kemalism called secularization of state and economy, and divorce of life from the universal moral laws of Shariat."

---

[15] Dhulipala, V, "A Nation State Insufficiently Imagined? Debating Pakistan in Late Colonial North India" (Indian Economic Social History Review, 2011): 377-405.

- ✓ He emphasized that as like Medina, Pakistan was the first step towards the greater Muslim *Ummah'* s rule in the world and like Medina will gradually flourish.

- ✓ He invoked the hostage population theory that If there will be Muslims left in Hindustan, There also will be Hindu minority in Pakistan and both will balance each other and ensure better conduct by respective Governments. In any case the minority Muslims will have in shape of Pakistan a safe haven where they can migrate in case of any problem in India.

V ANTI PAKISTAN POLITICAL PARTIES

Pakistan was not as much achieved by the All India Muslim League as much it was made possible by the Hindu and the British Opposition to the idea of Pakistan. In other words the propaganda for Pakistan was less effective than the propaganda Against Pakistan in making Muslim masses resolve hardened for the achievement of Pakistan. There were two categories of Parties opposing the idea of Pakistan or Partition of India. These were:

- **Nationwide Parties**
- **Regional Parties**

A NATIONWIDE PARTIES

a)   All India National Congress

From its foundation on 28 December 1885 until the time of independence of India on 15 August 1947, the Indian National Congress was the largest and most prominent Indian public organization, and central and defining influence of the Indian Independence Movement.[16]

---

[16] S. R, Bakshi, *Congress, Muslim League, and partition of India* (New Delhi: Deep & Deep Publications,1990), 156.

Congress was founded in 1885 to further the rights of all Indians. While Sir Syed Ahmed Khan persuaded the Muslims who followed him to stay aloof, some Muslims did join the Congress, including notably Badruddin Tyabjee and Mohammad Ali Jinnah himself. So long as the Congress believed in constitutional advancement and a top down approach to nation building, it remained an Indian party. Gandhi changed the nature of the Congress Party by taking it to the grassroots. Congress developed from its elite intellectual middle-class confines, and a moderate, loyalist agenda, to become by the inter-war years, a mass organisation. It was an organisation which, despite the tremendous diversity of the sub-continent, was remarkable in achieving broad consensus over the decades. Yet it was not a homogenous organisation and was often dominated by factionalism and opposing political strategies. This was exemplified by its splintering in 1907 into the so-called 'moderate' and 'extremist' wings of Gokhley and Tilak, which reunited 10 years later. Another example were the 'pro-changers' (who believed working the constitutional structures to weaken it from within) and 'no-changers' (who wanted to distance themselves from the Raj) during the 1920s. There was also a split within Congress between those who believed that violence was a justifiable weapon in the fight against imperial oppression (whose most iconic figure was Subhas Chandra Bose, who went on to form the Indian National Army), and those who stressed non-violence. The towering figure in this latter group was Mahatma Gandhi, who introduced a seismic new idiom of opposition in the shape of non-violent non-cooperation or 'satyagraha' (meaning 'truth' or 'soul' force'). [17]

Opposition to the Demand for Pakistan

The Hindu Myth of the Golden age of Vedas that was invoked to instill the pride of Nationalism in the Hindu became a bane between it and the other communities. This ideology was not closed to the communities outside the ambit of Hinduism but it required the other to give up their unique culture and adopt the Hindu Culture. This was particularly a cause of stress for the Muslims and played its part in their demand for the separate homeland.

The Congress and the Muslims had a long history, However the split occoured on the question of the Joint versus the separate electorates. The Congress wanted to gain independence of India and did not want to accept any demand for any separation from the united India. Congress considered the Muslim League as a pawn in British hands that wanted to leave the India divided and torn. Congress asserted and established it seal as a non communal party which was evident from its coalitions with the religious Jamiat ul Ulema e Hind, Jamat e Islami, Akali Dal , Khudai Khidmatgar and the Unionsit party of Punjab. Congress moreover rejected the theory of relative deprivation put forward by the Muslim League as in a Mulsilm Minority province as UP, Muslims being 14 percent of the Population controlled the 66% of the Land and occupied 40 percent of the posts in Judiciary and 255 percent of the posts in administrative setup.

---

[17] B. R Nanda, *Gandhi: pan-Islamism, imperialism, and nationalism in India* (Bombay: Oxford University Press, 1989), 158.

Similarly in case of Bengal whose Partition and subsequent re unification became a bitter strife between the Congress and the Muslim League have always had a Muslim Premier.

Muslims like Dr. Ansari and Maulan Abu Alkalam were one of the astute leaders of Congress. Maulan Abu Al Kalam was also very vocal against the Partition of India. His some famous arguments that also depict the voice of Congress are:

" I must confess that the very term Pakistan goes against my grain. It suggests that some portions of the world are pure while others are impure. Such a division of territories into pure and impure is un-Islamic...Furthermore, it seems that the scheme of Pakistan is a symbol of defeatism and has been built up on the analogy of the Jewish demand for a national home. It is a confession that Indian Muslims cannot hold of their own in India as a whole and would be content to withdraw to a corner specially reserved for them...."

"Over 90 million in number, they are in quantity and quality a sufficiently important element in Indian life to influence decisively all questions of administration and policy. Nature has further helped them by concentrating them in certain areas. In such a context, the demand for Pakistan looses all force. As a Muslim, I for one am not prepared for a moment to give up my right to treat the whole of India as my domain and share in the shaping of its political and economic life. To me it seems a sure sign of cowardice to give up what is my patrimony and content myself with a mere fragment of it."[18]

The Maulana then examines the consequences of partition quite objectively. Thus he says:

[18] Abūlkalām Āzād, *India wins freedom* (New York: Longmans, Green, 1960), 117.

"Let us consider dispassionately the consequences which will follow if we give effect to the Pakistan scheme. India will be divided into two states, one with a majority of Muslims and the other of Hindus. In the Hindustan State there will remain three and half crores of Muslims scattered in small minorities all over the land. With 17 per cent in U.P., 12 per cent in Bihar and 9 per cent in Madras, they will be weaker than they are today in the Hindu majority provinces. They have had their homelands in these regions for almost a thousand years and built up well known centers of Muslim culture and civilization there.

They will awaken overnight and discover that they have become alien and foreigners. Backward industrially, educationally and economically, they will be left to the mercies to what would become an unadulterated Hindu Raj.

On the other hand, their position within the Pakistan State will be vulnerable and weak. Nowhere in Pakistan will their majority be comparable to the Hindu majority in the Hindustan States.

In fact their majority will be so slight that it will be offset by the economical, educational and political lead enjoyed by non-Muslims in these areas. Even if this were not so and Pakistan were overwhelmingly Muslim in population, it still could hardly solve the problem of Muslims in Hindustan."

Also, the fear that if Pakistan is not formed the Centre with Hindu majority will interfere in Muslim majority provinces, Maulana counters by the argument (which was what the Cabinet Mission Plan was about) "The Congress meets this fear by granting full autonomy to the provinces. It has also provided for two lists of Central subjects, one compulsory and none optional so that if any provincial unit so wants, it can administer all subjects itself except a minimum delegated to the Centre. The Congress scheme, therefore ensures that Muslim majority provinces are internally free to develop as they will, but can at the same time influence the Centre on all issues which affect India as a whole."[19]

Congress till the end was against the creation of Pakistan , However in 1946 it consented for the partition of India and made creation of Pakistan possible.

---

[19] Abūlkalām Āzād, *India wins freedom* (New York: Longmans, Green, 1960), 129.

b)   Jamiat –Ul -Ulema-e-Hind (JUH)

Jamiat ul Ulema e Hind was created by Sheikh ul Hind Maulana Mehmood Hasan , Maulana Syed Hussain Madni, and other prominent Ulema of the time in 1919. This was the peak of the Khilafat Movement. After the demise of the Khilafat movement, the JUH became the political organ that trained the Muslim men in the theology and Islamic history. Jamiat ul Ulema e Hind had its influence spread all over the India. JUH took the stance that Hindu and Muslims were a composite Nation and propounded the theological basis for their nationalistic philosophy. It staunchly supported the All India National Congress in its opposition to Partition of India.

The JUH's major arguments against the Pakistan were: "The Pakistan demand has British support and is nothing but an instrument forged by them to further their policy of divide and rule; Pakistan will split and, therefore, weaken the Muslims in India; our real enemy is British imperialism and our only duty to defeat it, only a united action can achieve this; Muslims left behind India after separation will be at the mercy of the Hindus; partition will hinder the missionary activities of the Ulema; Muslim League leaders are ignorant of Islam, have no ideology, and are only exploiting the name of Islam for the worldly gain of Muslim vested interest; and Muslim League leaders are incapable of building up an Islamic state and their Pakistan will be no better than the Turkey of Mustafa Kamal".[20] The JUH formula conceived India as a loose Federation in which the provinces would be fully autonomous , granting only such powers to the Federal Government as they consent to. They proposed that freedom to religion will be protected as a fundamental right in the undivided India and all provinces could do legislation according to communal basis without federal interference.

[20] Dhulipala, V, "A Nation State Insufficiently Imagined? Debating Pakistan in Late Colonial North India" (Indian Economic Social History Review, 2011): 377-405.

In this regard the Critique done by the senior JUH Cleric Maulana Hafiz ur Rehman Seoharvi is considered to be one of the effective critiques of Pakistan. It came out on the eve of the 1945-1946 elections which became the referendum for Pakistan. It was published in form of Pamphlets and was carried out as a series of articles in a famous UP newspaper, *The Medina* .[21]

The main points of the argument are:

- ✓ The idea of Pakistan as a Muslim State is a sham as the minorities will get representation in the European style parliament in Pakistan where as in a true Islamic state Non- Muslims can only live as *Dhimmis* and have no role in the Government.

- ✓ The idea of population transfer will highly disturb the well being of the Muslims of the minority provinces which are after all the custodians of Muslim way of life.

- ✓ Pakistan will not be economically feasible with few natural resources and meager Capital. The Provinces of Pakistan have always been dependent on federal funding and will collapse in wake of the withdrawal.

- ✓ He further bemoaned the "Jinnah" and leaders of AIML such as "Sir Zafarullah" as *Qadiani*, and "Raja of Mehmoodabad" as *Shia* and dubbed all of them as worse than kafirs.

- ✓ Lastly he attacked the Pakistan from the standpoint of Urdu being its national language that will prompt the India to have *Devnagri Hindi* as its own and this will cause the death of Urdu in the Partitioned India.

---

[21] Ibid.

c)   Jamat e Islami (JI)

Jamaat-e-Islami was formed on 26 August 1941 at Lahore under the leadership of Sayyid Abul Ala Maududi. The objective of the Jamat was the 'Aqaamat e Deen" or "establishment of the Islamic way of life". It steadfastly opposed the idea of Pakistan or partition of India on basis of territorial boundaries.Maulana Maududi has been very vocal in his opposition to Pakistan. Some excrepts from his writings are as follows:

"In no Muslim League resolution, or in a speech by a responsible leader of the League it has it been made clear that their final goal is of establishing an Islamic system of government. Those who believe that by freeing Muslim majority areas rule of Hindu majority, an Islamic government will be established here in a democratic set up, are wrong. In fact what will be achieved will be a heretical government by Muslims, indeed worse than that." [22]

" Who are the Muslims you are claiming to be a separate nation? Here, the crowd called Muslims is full of all sorts of rabble. There are as many types of characters in this as in any (other) heathen people". [23]

"Pity! From League's Quaid-e-Azam down to the lower cadres, there is not a single person who has an Islamic outlook and thinking and whose perspective on matters is Islamic".[24]

[22] Sayed Riaz Ahmad, *Maulana Maududi and the Islamic state* (Lahore: People's Pub. House. 1976) , 123.

[23] *Ibid, 145.*

[24] Maulana Maududi, MUSLIMS AND THE PRESENT POLITICAL TURMOIL, (VOL.III) First Edition (Delhi, 1927), 1-56.

"To pronounce these people fit for leading Muslims for the simple reason that they are experts of Western type politics and masters of Western organizational arts, and are deeply in love with their people, is a manifestation of an un-Islamic viewpoint and reflects ignorance of Islam".[25]

One of the main arguments in favor of separate federations in India put up by Muslim League was that parliamentary democracy would not work in United India given the permanent minority that Muslims were with their own majority zones. Thus Pakistan – as a separate federation- had to be a democratic state. Jinnah's vision, as Gandhi concluded after his abortive meetings with Jinnah in 1944, was of a perfect democracy in Pakistan. This vision was rejected by Maulana Maududi and his party. The fact that Jinnah used electoral methods and strengths of numbers for his politics also upset Maulana Maududi quite a bit. He wrote:

"For these reasons, the great numbers (of Muslims) that we find. (listed) in the census records has become worthless for purposes of Islam. Anything done on the strength of these numbers will result in acute frustration." [26]

---

[25] Ibid.

[26] Ibid.

d)   Majlis-i-Ahrar-Islam Movement

The Majlis-i-Ahrar-Islam-Hind was founded in December 1929, at the time of the Congress session of 1929-30, in Lahore, during which the Congress had adopted a resolution for the complete independence of India. Persuaded by Maulana Abul Kalam Azad, some prominent Ulema (Muslim religious scholars) of India, mostly hailing from Punjab and led by Maulana Syed Ataullah Shah Bokhari, Chaudhry Afzal Haq, Maulana Zafar'Ali Khan and Maulana Mazhar Ali Azhar, established the Majlis-e-Ahrar Islam on 29 December 1929.[27] All the above-named leaders of the Majlis Ahrar had been very active in the Khilafat Movement. They had previously made important contributions to the Muslim cause in India in educational, religious and political fields. Majlis i Ahrar got famous for its strenuous anti Ahmadiya movement in 1931. This stance resulted into its clash with "All India Kashmir Committee" during the Kashmir uprising which had Sir Allama Muhammad Iqbal who was an *Ahmadi* till that time as its member.

---

[27] B. R Nanda, *Gandhi: pan-Islamism, imperialism, and nationalism in India* (Bombay: Oxford University Press, 1989), 160.

Majlis e Ahrar towed the Congress' s anti Pakistan stance due to its close affiliation with the Congress. Maulana Mazhar Ali Azhar wrote the famous couplet: "Ik Kafira kay peechay Islam ko chora, Yeh Quaid-e-Azam hai kay Kafir-e-Azam". Repeatedly Pakistan was described as "Palidistan", "Kafiristan" and "Khakistan" by the Majlis-e-Ahrar. Ironically, in 1946, its candidates were soundly defeated by the Muslim League's candidates.[28]

B   REGIONAL PARTIES

A number of regional parties also opposed the Partition of Provinces of India. Pakistan 's arduous opposition came from the province that had interestingly majority Muslim Population and numerous regional parties opposed the creation of Pakistan.

a)   Khudai Khidmatgar Movement

"Khudai Khidmatgar" movement also known as the "Red Shirts" was led by Khan Abdul Ghaffar Khan, known locally as Bacha Khan or Badshah Khan. By 1929 , The British Indian government made extensive propaganda against the Khudai Khidmatgars, and tried to equate them with the Bolsheviks, and even dubbed them as Russian agents, who intended to create anarchy and chaos in the country to destabilise the government — a charge always refuted by the Khudai Khidmatgars. [29]

---

[28] Khan Abdul Wali Khan, *Facts are facts: the untold story of India's partition* (New Delhi: Vikas Pub. House. 1987), 1-122.

[29] Ian Talbot, *Provincial politics and the Pakistan movement: the growth of the Muslim*

The most significant feature of the Khudai Khidmatgars was their adoption of non-violence and strict adherence to it. The volunteers were taught not to resort to violence and also not to carry weapons. The emphasis was on forbearance and tolerance. They were told not to retaliate, even if humiliated. Inspiration was provided by giving examples from the lives of Holy Prophet and his Companions. Ghaffar Khan also emphasised communal harmony in the province. Therefore, the membership was kept open to all, irrespective of any discrimination of caste, community or religion. Hence, a large number of non-Muslims joined the Khudai Khidmatgar organisation.

League in North-West and North-East India, 1937-1947 (Karachi: Oxford University Press, 1988), 1-178.

In December 1929, Ghaffar Khan and other prominent Khudai Khidmatgars attended the Lahore session of Indian National Congress. The Congress delegates met at the banks of river Ravi under the president ship of Pundit Jawaharlal Nehru and declared the complete independence for India as its goal. One of the main purposes of Abdul Ghaffar Khan and the Khudai Khidmatgars visiting Lahore and attending the Congress session was to draw the attention Indian public opinion to the 'cramped Frontier atmosphere'. They met the Congress leaders, apprised them of the current situation in the frontier and sought their help in this connection. The Congress high command promised to send a committee to enquire into their grievances. Ghaffar Khan was highly impressed by the enthusiasm and discipline of the Congress workers. On their return to the N-WFP, Ghaffar Khan and the rest of the Khudai Khidmatgars toured the entire province and organized people on the pattern of Congress organization. He also then came to be known as "Sarhadi Gandhi". Jirgas had been formed at village levels. Ghaffar Khan endorsed the Congress programme of complete independence and non-payment of taxes and revenues. This alliance of Congress and Khudai Khidmatgar was naturally not in favour of the partition of India on the basis of religion and gave a tough time to the Muslim League in the province. The Demand of the Khudai Khidmatgar was the creation of "Pukhtunistan" in event of Partition of India and they did not recognize the Durand line separating the NWPF from Afghanistan.

b)   Unionist Party of Punjab

The Unionist Party, a secular party, was formed to represent the interests of Punjab's large feudal classes and gentry. Sir Sikandar Hyat Khan, Sir Fazli Husain and Sir Chhotu Ram were the co-founders of the party. Although a majority of Unionists were Muslims, a large number of Hindus and Sikhs also supported and participated in the Unionist Party.[30]

---

[30] Ian Talbot, *Provincial politics and the Pakistan movement: the growth of the Muslim League in North-West and North-East India, 1937-1947* (Karachi: Oxford University Press, 1988), 1-178.

In contrast with the Indian National Congress and many other parties of the time, the Unionist Party did not have a mass-based approach. Also in contrast with Congress, the Unionists supported the British Raj, and contested elections for the Punjab Legislative Council and the central Legislative Council at a time when Congress and the Muslim League were boycotting them. As a result, the Unionist Party dominated the provincial legislature for a number of years, allowing an elected provincial government to function when other provinces were governed by direct rule. The main aim of Unionist Party was to safeguard the interests of land lords of Punjab and since Punjab was a Muslim majority area where Muslims were in Rule, They were not sympathetic to the cause of Pakistan. Although the famous Jinnah-Sikander Pact did become possible. The Unionist Muslims after the Jinnah-Sikandar Pact "were technically members of the League"[1] at that time as Ahmad Yar Daultana admitted in his letter to Jinnah, "I am a member of the Muslim League and my relations of loyalty with you will always remain un-shattered."[31]Sir Sikander Hayat khan (Premier of Punjab 1937 to 1942) however, was able to pull off his desired coalition with Indain national Congress and Akali Dal despite AIML 's opposition. The 1946 Elections however brought the downfall of the Unionist Party and it ceased to exist upon creation of Pakistan.

---

[31] Syed Sharifuddin, Pirzada, Foundations of Pakistan: All-India Muslim League documents, 1906-1947. Karachi: National Pub. House. 1969.

c)   Shiromani AkaliDal

Akali Dal was formed on December 20, 1920 as a task force of the Shiromani Gurudwara Prabandhak Committee, the Sikh religious body. The Akali Dal considers itself the principal representative of Sikhs. Sardar Sarmukh Singh Chubbal was the first president of a unified proper Akali Dal, but it became popular under Master Tara Singh.[32]

Lahore Resolution of 1940 had an immense political impact on the Punjab politics. In particular, the prospect of a Muslim homeland raised anxieties for the Sikh political leadership which by this time was dominated by the Shiromani Akali Dal. The Muslim-Sikh relations had been somewhat good but the Lahore Resolution of 1940 drew a hard-line and widened the gulf between the two communities even in the rural areas. To the Sikhs, the Pakistan scheme had ended any possibility of settlement with the Muslims. It created a crisis in the Punjab particularly in the Sikh politics. The Hindus adopted different styles of opposing the Pakistan scheme from different platforms nevertheless the strongest reaction came from the Sikh community because the Punjab, 'cornerstone' of the League's plan, was a sacred land of Sikhs. The All India Akali Conference was held at Attari (15 miles from Lahore) on 10-11 February 1940 in which the Akali Sikhs from all the parts of India participated. Isher Singh Majhail, Professor Ganga Singh, Santokh Singh, Sant Singh, MLA, and Partap Singh, MLA condemned the idea of a separate Muslim state.

On 31 March 1942, the Sikh All Parties Conference presented a memorandum to Cripps in which as usual they asked for the re-demarcation of the Punjab boundaries from the river Ravi to Delhi. The memorandum evaluated their services towards the British empire and their past political status in the Punjab. They also expressed their resentment on the points of Cripps proposals which undermined the Indian integrity and the Sikh position. In the memorandum, they presented facts and figures about the communal proportion in different areas of the Punjab. They maintained that originally Jhang and Multan districts and trans-Jhelum areas were not a part of the proper Punjab. They demanded not to include these areas into the Punjab. They contended that the Sikh population in the states was 2,600,000 which could further reduce the Muslim ratio. In the memorandum, they slipped from the demands to threats and expressed their anger that they were not considered justly by the British. They included the Sikh claims as under:

- ✓ From 25 to 33 per cent share in the Punjab cabinet and the Sikh representation
  should be compulsory in the cabinet,
- ✓ There should always be a coalition government in the Punjab,
- ✓ The Punjab be re-demarcated into two parts from the Ravi to Delhi consisting
  of Ambala and Jullundur Divisions and the districts of Lahore, Amritsar and
  Gurdaspur,

- ✓ The Sikhs be given weightage as the Muslims enjoyed in different provinces
  as minority.
  Five per cent representation in the centre,
- ✓ One Sikh minister in the central cabinet,
- ✓ Defence Advisory Committee be created with one Sikh seat in it,
- ✓ The Sikh status be maintained in the Indian defence forces,
- ✓ Sikh share in Indian and provincial services be maintained on existing lines or as the Muslims had in other minority provinces,
- ✓ Only the Sikh members would decide on the laws pertinent to the Sikh
  religion in the Legislature,
- ✓ The State would not interfere with the religious matters of the Sikhs,
- ✓ The Gurmukhi script would be introduced where necessary.[33]

The Sikh Memorandum also had an Annexure of the Muslim population in the Punjab districts according to 1931 census report. According to this Annexure, the Muslims had a clean majority in the western districts from Lahore to DG Khan while they had a slight majority (50.8%) in the Gurdaspur district. They also made reasonable percentage in rest of the eastern districts:

---

[33] Ian Talbot, *Provincial politics and the Pakistan movement: the growth of the Muslim League in North-West and North-East India, 1937-1947* (Karachi: Oxford University Press, 1988), 1-178.

DISTRICT	MUSLIM POPULATION
Amritsar	47%
Ferozepur	44.6%
Jullundur	44.5%
Hoshiarpur	31.8%
Ludhiana	35.1%

Source: Kirpal Singh, Partition of the Punjab, 21-22.[34]

Interestingly, they did not give the Sikh percentage in the same districts because without the other non-Muslim populations their claim to be a majority in the eastern districts had no importance. According to the *Eastern Times*, except Ludhiana the Sikhs were in a smaller proportion than the Muslim population in the eastern districts:

DISTRICT	SIKH POPULATION
Amritsar	35%
Ferozepur	33%
Jallandhur	26%
Ludhiana	46%

Source: The Eastern Times, 2 December 1942[35]

---

[34] Kirapāla Siṅgha. *The partition of the Punjab* (Patiala: Punjabi University, 1972),21-22.

[35] The Eastern Times, 2 December 1942

Except Ludhiana the Sikhs were in a smaller proportion than the Muslim population in the eastern districts. The Demands of AkaliDal were not accepted by the Cripps and its resentment towards the cause of Pakistan grew. Akali Dal called a meeting of the Sikhs in Amritsar in which Master Tara said that Pakistan was being imposed on the Sikhs but they were fully prepared to fight with the Muslims.[36]The Akalis pledged in a conference at Amritsar to make the Pakistan scheme a mere dream.

After the Cripps proposals, a letter by a Sikh was sent to Jinnah suggesting solution to the Sikh question. The writer explained that the Sikhs had been nobody in their own homeland before 1920s but they got prestige not on numerical basis but the military strength in the shape of the Akali Dal. The solution of the Muslim-Sikh problem was that a new state be created for Sikhs where all the communities should have balanced population. Otherwise, Pakistan was a matter of life and death for the Sikh community. The Sikhs were however confused among themselves and could not decide among themselves the course of action as the partition looms large. Parties other than the AkaliDal came into conflict over the requisite solution to the Sikh problem. The Sikh anxiety was about securing of their rights in a divided Punjab. However the problem was that Sikhs were very small in number as compared to the Muslims in the British Raj Punjab.

---

[36]T. Walter Wallbank, *The partition of India; causes and responsibilities* (Boston: Heath, 1966)

The Governor's reports in April 1941 depicted truly the contradicting attitude of the Sikh leadership:

"Akalis with Congress leanings consider that Sikhs should throw in their lot with Congress and concentrate on persuading it not to accept the scheme; Master Tara Singh and Giani Kartar Singh consider that an Akali-Hindu alliance offers the best chance of resistance; while Baba Kharak Singh considers that Akalis, instead becoming subservient to the Hindu Mahasabha, should attempt to enlist the sympathies of "nationalist" Muslims. Meanwhile, the Khalistan alternative is being kept in the background, though efforts continue to be made to arm the community and to place it on an organised and semi military basis on the plea of self-preservation."[37]

---

[37] Ian Talbot, *Provincial politics and the Pakistan movement: the growth of the Muslim League in North-West and North-East India, 1937-1947* (Karachi: Oxford University Press, 1988), 1-178.

d) Akhil Bhāratiya Hindū Mahāsabhā

In 1910, an All India Hindu Conference was organised in Allahabad by leading Hindu social and political leaders who sought to organise Indian Hindus politically in response to the rise of the Muslim League. The Hindu Mahasabha was founded in 1914 in Amritsar and established its headquarters in Haridwar. Despite its initial objective to be a Nationwide Party, it mostly remained a Northern India Party. Amongst its early leaders was the prominent nationalist and educationalist Pandit Madan Mohan Malaviya, who founded the Benaras Hindu University, and the Punjabi populist Lala Lajpat Rai. Under Malaviya, the Mahasabha campaigned for Hindu political unity, for the education and economic development of Hindus as well as for the reconversion of Muslims to Hinduism.

While not loyal to the British Raj, the Hindu Mahasabha did not actively support agitations against British rule in India. Although the Hindu Mahasabha did not call for the exclusion of other religious communities from government, it identified India as a "Hindu Rashtra" (Hindu Nation) and believed in the primacy of Hindu culture, religion and heritage. The Mahasabha advocates that Sikhs, Jains and Buddhists are also Hindu in terms of national and political identity. It argues that Islam and Christianity are foreign religions, with their holy places being in Arabia, Palestine and Rome, and that Indian Muslims and Christians are simply descendants of Hindus who were converted by force, coercion and bribery. At various points in its history, the party called for the re-conversion of Muslims and Christians to Hinduism. The Hindu Mahasabha stridently opposes Westernization, which it regards as a decadent influence on Indian youth and culture. It calls for a revival of the Sanskrit language and the primacy of Hindi. The Mahasabha opposed socialism and communism as decadent foreign ideologies that do not represent India's indigenous needs and conditions.[38] Its ideology naturally made it the opposition to the Idea of Pakistan. The Mahasaba however remained at the margins of the Politics and was shadowed by the Rashteriya Swayamsewak Sangh.

---

[38] Mānikacandra Vājapeyī and Śrīdhara Parāḍakara, *Partition-days: the fiery saga of RSS* (New Delhi: Suruchi Prakashan, 2002), 1-104.

e)   Rashteriya Swayamsewak Sangh

The RSS portrayed itself as a social movement rather than a political party, and did not play any central role in the Indian independence movement. K. B. Hedgewar, its first chief, had been imprisoned in 1921 for anti-British activities. However, after the formation of RSS in 1925, he refrained from getting involved in such activities except the Jangal Satyagraha, which he participated in with the goal of meeting potential RSS members. In 1930, he told the RSS cadres that they could join Gandhi's Salt Satyagraha, but RSS would not participate in it as an organization. When the Congress passed the Purna Swaraj resolution in 1930, he asked all the RSS branches hoist the Indian flag and organize lectures on the need of independence. However, the RSS emphatically rejected the Congress policy of cooperation with the Miuslims. Subsequently, in 1934, the Congress banned its members from joining RSS, Hindu Mahasabha or Muslim League.

The RSS policy of not participating in any anti-British activities continued after M. S. Golwalkar became its chief in 1940. Golwalkar did not want to give the British any excuse to ban the RSS. After the Muslim League passed the Lahore Resolution demanding a separate Pakistan, the RSS campaigned for a Hindu nation, but stayed away from the independence struggle. When the British Government banned military drills and use of uniforms in non-official organizations, Golwalkar terminated the RSS military department. RSS also stayed away from the Quit India Movement and the naval revolt, although it played an important role in anti-Muslim violence during the Partition of India in 1947.

According to an internal Congress report published in 1947, RSS remained primarily a Maharashtrian Brahmin organization, with no mass presence in politics even in the Marathi-speaking areas. [39]

[39] Mānikacandra Vājapeyī and Śrīdhara Parāḍakara, *Partition-days: the fiery saga of RSS* (New Delhi: Suruchi Prakashan, 2002), 1-104.

VI) CONCLUSION

A student of history may ask: who was the architect of partition? Iqbal? Jinnah? Gandhi? Nehru? Patel? The Congress party? The Muslim League? The Hindu Mahasabha? The Akali Dal? The British? No one person and no single party can take the credit or the blame for partition. It was a deadly serious game that had many players. The principal figures involved have acquired an iconic status in India and Pakistan. Often the hero of one is a villain for the other, so bitter was the experience of partition. Sixty years later, when one looks at them as historical figures, one finds them to be all too human, with their prides and their prejudices, their strengths and their limitations. They made choices like all humans and these choices had the human touch of triumph and tragedy. They were as much creators of history as were its victims.

It has been argued that the concept of the "United India" as created by the British Raj had never existed in the history of India. India had always remained as a loose confederation of states even in the times of the great Kanishka Dynasty and the Great Moghul empire under Emporer Akbar that ruled over the present day India, Pakistan and Bangladesh. The British Raj came and gave the idea of caste and creed and widened the cleavage between the different cultures living side by side in India. The political system it introduced to gain collaborators evolved and then stood against it. The Political values that it had instilled into the Indian Elite and Middle Class then made the outlook of the respective Political parties on the basis of their perceived ideology. The ideology started from being the Nationalist, freedom of India Demand to the more specific demand of Partition of India on communal basis between the Hindus and Muslims on the basis of Two nation theory.

There emerged three groups of actors at the chess board of India striving for freedom from the British Raj. These groups were the Nationalist Parties led by the Congress, The Regional Parties and The Muslim League. The easier are to understand the motives of the regional parties that kept un naturally in unitary system naturally wanted to gain their separate status. The Congress was the oldest among all these parties and most of the Leaders including Jinnah of the All India Muslim League had been part of the Congress. Congress had strived to become a non communal an all Indian representative Political party and considered a united India as the resurrection of its golden past . The Muslim league on the other hand, represented the communal interests of the interestingly the Muslim minority provinces since it was conceived in Bengal and rallied on the support of the Muslims from these provinces. Muslims by the time of the Lahore Resolution, and passed through the humiliating treatment in renunciation of division of Bengal, the loss of the Nominal Khilafat of the Ottoman Empire at the hands of the British and the Conduct of Congress towards the Demand of Muslim ministries in aftermath of 1937   Election loss. In this regard Elections of 1937 became a turning point in the Consolidation of Demand of Pakistan by the Muslim league and its subsequent Opposition. The Muslim League understood that in order to gain prominence it had to use the slogan of Religion, the real motive was to get a Pakistan that could host the Community of Muslims and not Islam. However in absence of the support of the largely Deoband Ulema, Muslim League had to rely heavily on the slogan of Pakistan as being the only choice for Muslims. This propaganda might not have made possible the creation of Pakistan if it was not as vehemently refuted by the Congress led galaxy of nationwide, religious and the regional Parties. This opposition created in the mind of Muslim masses the fear that Pakistan is something very much against the Hindu extremist ideology and the proper retreat of the Muslims. By the time of the Cripps Mission in 1942, the India had divided itself on the Communal basis as clearly drawing lines between the two distinct communities of India: The Hindu and The Muslim. Attempts at reconciliation in form of the Delhi proposals of Jinnah and Gandhi-Jinnah dialogue were thwarted by the general environment of the rhetoric that had been created on the communal lines. The leaders like Maulana Abu al Kalam , Jawahar Lal Nehru tried to address the rhetoric of Pakistan till the last time but it did not turn the tide of the Muslim League and it won overwhelming majority in the 1946 Elections which proved to be the referendum for Pakistan. This Victory made some of the prominent Political parties like Jamat e Islami, Khudai Khidmatgar, Khaksar Movement and the Unionist Party of Punjab to join the newly created state of Pakistan despite their underlying opposition to the idea of separation.

BIBLIOGRAPHY

Ahmad, Sayed Riaz. 1976. Maulana Maududi and the Islamic state. Lahore: People's Pub. House.

Āzād, Abūlkalām. 1960. India wins freedom. New York: Longmans, Green.

Bakshi, S. R. 1990. Congress, Muslim League, and partition of India. New Delhi: Deep & Deep Publications

Cohen, S.P. 2004. The Idea of Pakistan. Washington D.C.: Brookings Institution Press.

Dhulipala, V. 2011. A Nation State Insufficiently Imagined? Debating Pakistan in Late Colonial North India. Indian Economic Social History Review, 48 (3), pp. 377-405.

Inder Singh, Anita. 1987. The origins of the partition of India, 1936-1947. Delhi: Oxford University Press.

Jalal, A. 1985. The Sole Spokesman: Jinnah, the Muslim League and the Pakistan Demand. Cambridge: Cambridge University Press.

Kirapāla Siṅgha. 1972. The partition of the Punjab. Patiala: Punjabi University.

More, J. B. P. 2008. Partition of India: players and partners. Kannur: Institute for Research in Social Sciences & Humanities.

MRT. 1992. Pakistan and Muslim India. Karachi: Urdu Academy Sind for the Toosy Foundation

Nanda, B. R. 1989. Gandhi: pan-Islamism, imperialism, and nationalism in India. Bombay: Oxford University Press.

Pirzada, Syed Sharifuddin. 1969. Foundations of Pakistan: All-India Muslim League documents, 1906-1947. Karachi: National Pub. House.

Shaikh, F. 2009. Making Sense of Pakistan. London: Hurst & Company.

Talbot, Ian. 1988. Provincial politics and the Pakistan movement: the growth of the Muslim League in North-West and North-East India, 1937-1947. Karachi: Oxford University Press.

Wali Khan, Khan Abdul. 1987. Facts are facts: the untold story of India's partition. New Delhi: Vikas Pub. House.

Wallbank, T. Walter. 1966. The partition of India; causes and responsibilities. Boston: Heath.

Zamindar, V.F. 2007 The Long Partition and the Making of Modern South Asia: Refugees, Boundaries, Histories. New York: Columbia University Press.

ANNEXURE-I

LAHORE RESOLUTION

1. While approving and endorsing the action taken by the Council and the Working Committee of the All-India Muslim League, as indicated in their resolutions dated the 27th of August, 17th and 18th of September and 22nd of October, 1939, and 3rd of February 1940, on the constitutional issue, this session of the All-India Muslim League emphatically reiterates that the scheme of Federation embodied in the Government of India Act, 1935 is totally unsuited to, and unworkable in the peculiar conditions of this country and is altogether unacceptable to Muslim India.

2. It further records its emphatic view that while the declaration dated the 18th of October, 1939, made by the Viceroy on behalf of His Majesty's Government is reassuring in so far as it declares that the policy and plan on which the Government of India Act, 1935 is based will be reconsidered in consultation with the various parties, interests and communities in India, Muslim India will not be satisfied unless the whole constitutional plan is reconsidered de novo and that no revised plan would be acceptable to the Muslims unless it is framed with their approval and consent.

3. Resolved that it is the considered view of this session of the All-India Muslim League that no constitutional plan would be workable in this country or acceptable to Muslims unless it is designed on the following basic principle, namely, that geographically contiguous units are demarcated into regions which should be so constituted, with such territorial readjustments as may be necessary, that the areas in which the Muslims are numerically in a majority, as in the North-Western and Eastern Zones of India, should be grouped to constitute 'Independent States' in which the constituent units shall be autonomous and sovereign.

That adequate, effective and mandatory safeguards should be specifically provided in the constitution for minorities in these units and in these regions for the protection of their religious, cultural, economic, political, administrative and other rights and interests in consultation with them; and in other parts of India where Mussalmans are in a minority, adequate, effective and mandatory safeguard shall be specially provided in the constitution for them and other minorities for the protection of their religious, cultural, economic, political, administrative and other rights and interests in consultation with them.

This session further authorizes the Working Committee to frame a scheme of constitution in accordance with these basic principles, providing for the assumption finally by the respective regions of all powers such as defence, external affairs, communications, customs and such other matters as may be necessary.

Source: Resolutions of the All-India Muslim League: From December 1938 to March 1940, pub. Liaquat Ali khan (Delhi, n.d.), pp. 47-9.

ANNEXURE II

Sir Muhammad Iqbal's 1930 Presidential Address to the 25th Session of the All-India Muslim League Allahabad, 29 December 1930

[[1]] Islam and Nationalism

[[2]] The Unity of an Indian Nation

[[3]] Muslim India Within India

[[4]] Federal States

[[5]] Federation As Understood in the Simon Report

[[6]] Federal Scheme As Discussed in the Round Table Conference

[[7]] The Problem of Defence

[[8]] The Alternative

[[9]] The Round Table Conference

[[10]] The Conclusion

[[0]] Gentlemen, I am deeply grateful to you for the honour you have conferred upon me in inviting me to preside over the deliberations of the All-India Muslim League at one of the most critical moments in the history of Muslim political thought and activity in India. I have no doubt that in this great assembly there are men whose political experience is far more extensive than mine, and for whose knowledge of affairs I have the highest respect. It will, therefore, be presumptuous on my part to claim to guide an assembly of such men in the political decisions which they are called upon to make today. I lead no party; I follow no leader. I have given the best part of my life to a careful study of Islam, its law and polity, its culture, its history and its literature. This constant contact with the spirit of Islam, as it unfolds itself in time, has, I think, given me a kind of insight into its significance as a world fact. It is in the light of this insight, whatever its value, that, while assuming that the Muslims of India are determined to remain true to the spirit of Islam, I propose not to guide you in your decisions, but to attempt the humbler task of bringing clearly to your consciousness the main principle which, in my opinion, should determine the general character of these decisions.

[[1]] Islam and Nationalism

[[1a]] It cannot be denied that Islam, regarded as an ethical ideal plus a certain kind of polity – by which expression I mean a social structure regulated by a legal system and animated by a specific ethical ideal – has been the chief formative factor in the life-history of the Muslims of India. It has furnished those basic emotions and loyalties which gradually unify scattered individuals and groups, and finally transform them into a well-defined people, possessing a moral consciousness of their own. Indeed it is not an exaggeration to say that India is perhaps the only country in the world where Islam, as a people-building force, has worked at its best. In India, as elsewhere, the structure of Islam as a society is almost entirely due to the working of Islam as a culture inspired by a specific ethical ideal. What I mean to say is that Muslim society, with its remarkable homogeneity and inner unity, has grown to be what it is, under the pressure of the laws and institutions associated with the culture of Islam.

[[1b]] The ideas set free by European political thinking, however, are now rapidly changing the outlook of the present generation of Muslims both in India and outside India. Our younger men, inspired by these ideas, are anxious to see them as living forces in their own countries, without any critical appreciation of the facts which have determined their evolution in Europe. In Europe Christianity was understood to be a purely monastic order which gradually developed into a vast church organisation. The protest of Luther was directed against this church organisation, not against any system of polity of a secular nature, for the obvious reason that there was no such polity associated with Christianity. And Luther was perfectly justified in rising in revolt against this organisation; though, I think, he did not realise that in the peculiar conditions which obtained in Europe, his revolt would eventually mean the complete displacement of [the] universal ethics of Jesus by the growth of a plurality of national and hence narrower systems of ethics.

[[1c]] Thus the upshot of the intellectual movement initiated by such men as Rousseau and Luther was the break-up of the one into [the] mutually ill-adjusted many, the transformation of a human into a national outlook, requiring a more realistic foundation, such as the notion of country, and finding expression through varying systems of polity evolved on national lines, i.e. on lines which recognise territory as the only principle of political solidarity. If you begin with the conception of religion as complete other-worldliness, then what has happened to Christianity in Europe is perfectly natural. The universal ethics of Jesus is displaced by national systems of ethics and polity. The conclusion to which Europe is consequently driven is that religion is a private affair of the individual and has nothing to do with what is called man's temporal life.

[[1d]] Islam does not bifurcate the unity of man into an irreconcilable duality of spirit and matter. In Islam God and the universe, spirit and matter, Church and State, are organic to each other. Man is not the citizen of a profane world to be renounced in the interest of a world of spirit situated elsewhere. To Islam, matter is spirit realising itself in space and time. Europe uncritically accepted the duality of spirit and matter, probably from Manichaean thought. Her best thinkers are realising this initial mistake today, but her statesmen are indirectly forcing the world to accept it as an unquestionable dogma. It is, then, this mistaken separation of spiritual and temporal which has largely influenced European religious and political thought and has resulted practically in the total exclusion of Christianity from the life of European States. The result is a set of mutually ill-adjusted States dominated by interests not human but national. And these mutually ill-adjusted States, after trampling over the moral and religious convictions of Christianity, are today feeling the need of a federated Europe, i.e. the need of a unity which the Christian church organisation originally gave them, but which, instead of reconstructing it in the light of Christ's vision of human brotherhood, they considered fit to destroy under the inspiration of Luther.

[[1e]] A Luther in the world of Islam, however, is an impossible phenomenon; for here there is no church organisation similar to that of Christianity in the Middle Ages, inviting a destroyer. In the world of Islam we have a universal polity whose fundamentals are believed to have been revealed but whose structure, owing to our legists' [=legal theorists'] want of contact with the modern world, today stands in need of renewed power by fresh adjustments. I do not know what will be the final fate of the national idea in the world of Islam. Whether Islam will assimilate and transform it, as it has before assimilated and transformed many ideas expressive of a different spirit, or allow a radical transformation of its own structure by the force of this idea, is hard to predict. Professor Wensinck of Leiden (Holland) wrote to me the other day: "It seems to me that Islam is entering upon a crisis through which Christianity has been passing for more than a century. The great difficulty is how to save the foundations of religion when many antiquated notions have to be given up. It seems to me scarcely possible to state what the outcome will be for Christianity, still less what it will be for Islam." At the present moment the national idea is racialising the outlook of Muslims, and thus materially counteracting the humanizing work of Islam. And the growth of racial consciousness may mean the growth of standards different [from] and even opposed to the standards of Islam.

[[1f]] I hope you will pardon me for this apparently academic discussion. To address this session of the All-India Muslim League you have selected a man who is [=has] not despaired of Islam as a living force for freeing the outlook of man from its geographical limitations, who believes that religion is a power of the utmost importance in the life of individuals as well as States, and finally who believes that Islam is itself Destiny and will not suffer a destiny. Such a man cannot but look at matters from his own point of view. Do not think that the problem I am indicating is a purely theoretical one. It is a very living and practical problem calculated to affect the very fabric of Islam as a system of life and conduct. On a proper solution of it alone depends your future as a distinct cultural unit in India. Never in our history has Islam had to stand a greater trial than the one which confronts it today. It is open to a people to modify, reinterpret or reject the foundational principles of their social structure; but it is absolutely necessary for them to see clearly what they are doing before they undertake to try a fresh experiment. Nor should the way in which I am approaching this important problem lead anybody to think that I intend to quarrel with those who happen to think differently. You are a Muslim assembly and, I suppose, anxious to remain true to the spirit and ideals of Islam. My sole desire, therefore, is to tell you frankly what I honestly believe to be the truth about the present situation. In this way alone it is possible for me to illuminate, according to my light, the avenues of your political action.

[[2]] The Unity of an Indian Nation

[[2a]] What, then, is the problem and its implications? Is religion a private affair? Would you like to see Islam as a moral and political ideal, meeting the same fate in the world of Islam as Christianity has already met in Europe? Is it possible to retain Islam as an ethical ideal and to reject it as a polity, in favor of national polities in which [the] religious attitude is not permitted to play any part? This question becomes of special importance in India, where the Muslims happen to be a minority. The proposition that religion is a private individual experience is not surprising on the lips of a European. In Europe the conception of Christianity as a monastic order, renouncing the world of matter and fixing its gaze entirely on the world of spirit, led, by a logical process of thought, to the view embodied in this proposition. The nature of the Prophet's religious experience, as disclosed in the Quran, however, is wholly different. It is not mere experience in the sense of a purely biological event, happening inside the experient and necessitating no reactions on its social environment. It is individual experience creative of a social order. Its immediate outcome is the fundamentals of a polity with implicit legal concepts whose civic significance cannot be belittled merely because their origin is revelational.

[[2b]] The religious ideal of Islam, therefore, is organically related to the social order which it has created. The rejection of the one will eventually involve the rejection of the other. Therefore the construction of a polity on national lines, if it means a displacement of the Islamic principle of solidarity, is simply unthinkable to a Muslim. This is a matter which at the present moment directly concerns the Muslims of India. "Man," says Renan, "is enslaved neither by his race, nor by his religion, nor by the course of rivers, nor by the direction of mountain ranges. A great aggregation of men, sane of mind and warm of heart, creates a moral consciousness which is called a nation." Such a formation is quite possible, though it involves the long and arduous process of practically remaking men and furnishing them with a fresh emotional equipment. It might have been a fact in India if the teaching of Kabir and the Divine Faith of Akbar had seized the imagination of the masses of this country. Experience, however, shows that the various caste units and religious units in India have shown no inclination to sink their respective individualities in a larger whole. Each group is intensely jealous of its collective existence. The formation of the kind of moral consciousness which constitutes the essence of a nation in Renan's sense demands a price which the peoples of India are not prepared to pay.

[[2c]] The unity of an Indian nation, therefore, must be sought not in the negation, but in the mutual harmony and cooperation, of the many. True statesmanship cannot ignore facts, however unpleasant they may be. The only practical course is not to assume the existence of a state of things which does not exist, but to recognise facts as they are, and to exploit them to our greatest advantage. And it is on the discovery of Indian unity in this direction that the fate of India as well as of Asia really depends. India is Asia in miniature. Part of her people have cultural affinities with nations of the east, and part with nations in the middle and west of Asia. If an effective principle of cooperation is discovered in India, it will bring peace and mutual goodwill to this ancient land which has suffered so long, more because of her situation in historic space than because of any inherent incapacity of her people. And it will at the same time solve the entire political problem of Asia.

[[2d]] It is, however, painful to observe that our attempts to discover such a principle of internal harmony have so far failed. Why have they failed? Perhaps we suspect each other's intentions and inwardly aim at dominating each other. Perhaps, in the higher interests of mutual cooperation, we cannot afford to part with the monopolies which circumstances have placed in our hands, and [thus we] conceal our egoism under the cloak of nationalism, outwardly simulating a large-hearted patriotism, but inwardly as narrow-minded as a caste or tribe. Perhaps we are unwilling to recognise that each group has a right to free development according to its own cultural traditions. But whatever may be the causes of our failure, I still feel hopeful. Events seem to be tending in the direction of some sort of internal harmony. And as far as I have been able to read the Muslim mind, I have no hesitation in declaring that if the principle that the Indian Muslim is entitled to full and free development on the lines of his own culture and tradition in his own Indian home-lands is recognized as the basis of a permanent communal settlement, he will be ready to stake his all for the freedom of India.

[[2e]] The principle that each group is entitled to its free development on its own lines is not inspired by any feeling of narrow communalism. There are communalisms and communalisms. A community which is inspired by feelings of ill-will towards other communities is low and ignoble. I entertain the highest respect for the customs, laws, religious and social institutions of other communities. Nay, it is my duty, according to the teaching of the Quran, even to defend their places of worship, if need be. Yet I love the communal group which is the source of my life and behaviour; and which has formed me what I am by giving me its religion, its literature, its thought, its culture, and thereby recreating its whole past as a living operative factor, in my present consciousness. Even the authors of the Nehru Report recognise the value of this higher aspect of communalism. While discussing the separation of Sind they say, "To say from the larger viewpoint of nationalism that no communal provinces should be created, is, in a way, equivalent to saying from the still wider international viewpoint that there should be no separate nations. Both these statements have a measure of truth in them. But the staunchest internationalist recognises that without the fullest national autonomy it is extraordinarily difficult to create the international State. So also without the fullest cultural autonomy – and communalism in its better aspect is culture – it will be difficult to create a harmonious nation."

[[3]] Muslim India Within India

[[3a]] Communalism in its higher aspect, then, is indispensable to the formation of a harmonious whole in a country like India. The units of Indian society are not territorial as in European countries. India is a continent of human groups belonging to different races, speaking different languages, and professing different religions. Their behaviour is not at all determined by a common race-consciousness. Even the Hindus do not form a homogeneous group. The principle of European democracy cannot be applied to India without recognising the fact of communal groups. The Muslim demand for the creation of a Muslim India within India is, therefore, perfectly justified. The resolution of the All-Parties Muslim Conference at Delhi is, to my mind, wholly inspired by this noble ideal of a harmonious whole which, instead of stifling the respective individualities of its component wholes, affords them chances of fully working out the possibilities that may be latent in them. And I have no doubt that this House will emphatically endorse the Muslim demands embodied in this resolution.

[[3b]] Personally, I would go farther than the demands embodied in it. I would like to see the Punjab, North-West Frontier Province, Sind and Baluchistan amalgamated into a single State. Self-government within the British Empire, or without the British Empire, the formation of a consolidated North-West Indian Muslim State appears to me to be the final destiny of the Muslims, at least of North-West India. The proposal was put forward before the Nehru Committee. They rejected it on the ground that, if carried into effect, it would give a very unwieldy State. This is true in so far as the area is concerned; in point of population, the State contemplated by the proposal would be much less than some of the present Indian provinces. The exclusion of Ambala Division, and perhaps of some districts where non-Muslims predominate, will make it less extensive and more Muslim in population – so that the exclusion suggested will enable this consolidated State to give a more effective protection to non-Muslim minorities within its area. The idea need not alarm the Hindus or the British. India is the greatest Muslim country in the world. The life of Islam as a cultural force in the country very largely depends on its centralisation in a specified territory. This centralisation of the most living portion of the Muslims of India, whose military and police service has, notwithstanding unfair treatment from the British, made the British rule possible in this country, will eventually solve the problem of India as well as of Asia. It will intensify their sense of responsibility and deepen their patriotic feeling.

[[3c]] Thus, possessing full opportunity of development within the body politic of India, the North-West Indian Muslims will prove the best defenders of India against a foreign invasion, be that invasion one of ideas or of bayonets. The Punjab with 56 percent Muslim population supplies 54 percent of the total combatant troops in the Indian Army, and if the 19,000 Gurkhas recruited from the independent State of Nepal are excluded, the Punjab contingent amounts to 62 percent of the whole Indian Army. This percentage does not take into account nearly 6,000 combatants supplied to the Indian Army by the North-West Frontier Province and Baluchistan. From this you can easily calculate the possibilities of North-West Indian Muslims in regard to the defence of India against foreign aggression. The Right Hon'ble Mr. Srinivasa Sastri thinks that the Muslim demand for the creation of autonomous Muslim states along the north-west border is actuated by a desire "to acquire means of exerting pressure in emergencies on the Government of India." I may frankly tell him that the Muslim demand is not actuated by the kind of motive he imputes to us; it is actuated by a genuine desire for free development which is practically impossible under the type of unitary government contemplated by the nationalist Hindu politicians with a view to secure permanent communal dominance in the whole of India.

[[3d]] Nor should the Hindus fear that the creation of autonomous Muslim states will mean the introduction of a kind of religious rule in such states. I have already indicated to you the meaning of the word religion, as applied to Islam. The truth is that Islam is not a Church. It is a State conceived as a contractual organism long before Rousseau ever thought of such a thing, and animated by an ethical ideal which regards man not as an earth-rooted creature, defined by this or that portion of the earth, but as a spiritual being understood in terms of a social mechanism, and possessing rights and duties as a living factor in that mechanism. The character of a Muslim State can be judged from what the Times of India pointed out some time ago in a leader [=front-page article] on the Indian Banking Inquiry Committee. "In ancient India," the paper points out, "the State framed laws regulating the rates of interest; but in Muslim times, although Islam clearly forbids the realisation of interest on money loaned, Indian Muslim States imposed no restrictions on such rates." I therefore demand the formation of a consolidated Muslim State in the best interests of India and Islam. For India, it means security and peace resulting from an internal balance of power; for Islam, an opportunity to rid itself of the stamp that Arabian Imperialism was forced to give it, to mobilise its law, its education, its culture, and to bring them into closer contact with its own original spirit and with the spirit of modern times.

[[4]] Federal States

[[4a]] Thus it is clear that in view of India's infinite variety in climates, races, languages, creeds and social systems, the creation of autonomous States, based on the unity of language, race, history, religion and identity of economic interests, is the only possible way to secure a stable constitutional structure in India. The conception of federation underlying the Simon Report necessitates the abolition of the Central Legislative Assembly as a popular assembly, and makes it an assembly of the representatives of federal States. It further demands a redistribution of territory on the lines which I have indicated. And the Report does recommend both. I give my wholehearted support to this view of the matter, and venture to suggest that the redistribution recommended in the Simon Report must fulfill two conditions. It must precede the introduction of the new constitution, and must be so devised as to finally solve the communal problem. Proper redistribution will make the question of joint and separate electorates automatically disappear from the constitutional controversy of India. It is the present structure of the provinces that is largely responsible for this controversy.

[[4b]] The Hindu thinks that separate electorates are contrary to the spirit of true nationalism, because he understands the word nation to mean a kind of universal amalgamation in which no communal entity ought to retain its private individuality. Such a state of things, however, does not exist. Nor is it desirable that it should exist. India is a land of racial and religious variety. Add to this the general economic inferiority of the Muslims, their enormous debt, especially in the Punjab, and their insufficient majorities in some of the provinces as at present constituted, and you will begin to see clearly the meaning of our anxiety to retain separate electorates. In such a country and in such circumstances territorial electorates cannot secure adequate representation of all interests, and must inevitably lead to the creation of an oligarchy. The Muslims of India can have no objection to purely territorial electorates if provinces are demarcated so as to secure comparatively homogeneous communities possessing linguistic, racial, cultural and religious unity.

[[5]] Federation As Understood in the Simon Report

[[5a]] But in so far as the question of the powers of the Central Federal State is concerned, there is a subtle difference of motive in the constitutions proposed by the pundits of India and the pundits of England. The pundits of India do not disturb the Central authority as it stands at present. All that they desire is that this authority should become fully responsible to the Central Legislature which they maintain intact and where their majority will become further reinforced on the nominated element ceasing to exist. The pundits of England, on the other hand, realising that democracy in the Centre tends to work contrary to their interests and is likely to absorb the whole power now in their hands, in case a further advance is made towards responsible government, have shifted the experience of democracy from the Centre to the provinces. No doubt, they introduce the principle of Federation and appear to have made a beginning by making certain proposals; yet their evaluation of this principle is determined by considerations wholly different to those which determine its value in the eyes of Muslim India. The Muslims demand federation because it is pre-eminently a solution of India's most difficult problem, i.e. the communal problem. The Royal Commissioners' view of federation, though sound in principle, does not seem to aim at responsible government for federal States. Indeed it does not go beyond providing means of escape from the situation which the introduction of democracy in India has created for the British, and wholly disregards the communal problem by leaving it where it was.

[[5b]] Thus it is clear that, in so far as real federation is concerned, the Simon Report virtually negatives the principle of federation in its true significance. The Nehru Report, realising [a] Hindu majority in the Central Assembly, reaches a unitary form of government because such an institution secures Hindu dominance throughout India; the Simon Report retains the present British dominance behind the thin veneer of an unreal federation, partly because the British are naturally unwilling to part with the power they have so long wielded and partly because it is possible for them, in the absence of an inter-communal understanding in India, to make out a plausible case for the retention of that power in their own hands. To my mind a unitary form of government is simply unthinkable in a self-governing India. What is called "residuary powers" must be left entirely to self-governing States, the Central Federal State exercising only those powers which are expressly vested in it by the free consent of federal States. I would never advise the Muslims of India to agree to a system, whether of British or of Indian origin, which virtually negatives the principle of true federation, or fails to recognise them as a distinct political entity.

[[6]] Federal Scheme As Discussed in the Round Table Conference

[[6a]] The necessity for a structural change in the Central Government was seen probably long before the British discovered the most effective means for introducing this change. That is why at rather a late stage it was announced that the participation of the Indian Princes in the Round Table Conference was essential. It was a kind of surprise to the people of India, particularly the minorities, to see the Indian Princes dramatically expressing their willingness at the Round Table Conference to join an all-India federation and, as a result of their declaration, Hindu delegates – uncompromising advocates of a unitary form of government – quietly agreeing to the evolution of a federal scheme. Even Mr. Sastri who only a few days before had severely criticised Sir John Simon for recommending a federal scheme for India, suddenly became a convert and admitted his conversion in the plenary session of the Conference – thus offering the Prime Minister of England an occasion for one of his wittiest observations in his concluding speech. All this has a meaning both for the British who have sought the participation of the Indian Princes, and for the Hindus who have unhesitatingly accepted the evolution of an all-India federation. The truth is that the participation of the Indian Princes, among whom only a few are Muslims, in a federation scheme serves a double purpose. On the one hand, it serves as an all-important factor in maintaining the British power in India practically as it is; on the other hand, it gives [an] overwhelming majority to the Hindus in an All-India Federal Assembly.

[[6b]] It appears to me that the Hindu-Muslim differences regarding the ultimate form of the Central Government are being cleverly exploited by British politicians through the agency of the Princes who see in the scheme prospects of better security for their despotic rule. If the Muslims silently agree to any such scheme, it will simply hasten their end as a political entity in India. The policy of the Indian federation thus created, will be practically controlled by [the] Hindu Princes forming the largest group in the Central Federal Assembly. They will always lend their support to the Crown in matters of Imperial concern; and in so far as internal administration of the country is concerned, they will help in maintaining and strengthening the supremacy of the Hindus. In other words, the scheme appears to be aiming at a kind of understanding between Hindu India and British Imperialism – you perpetuate me in India, and I in return give you a Hindu oligarchy to keep all other Indian communities in perpetual subjection. If, therefore, the British Indian provinces are not transformed into really autonomous States, the Princes' participation in a scheme of Indian federation will be interpreted only as a dexterous move on the part of British politicians to satisfy, without parting with any real power, all parties concerned – Muslims with the word federation; Hindus with a majority in the Centre; the British Imperialists – with the substance of real power.

[[6c]] The number of Hindu States in India is far greater than Muslim States; and it remains to be seen how the Muslim demand for 33 percent [of the] seats in the Central Federal Assembly is to be met within a House or Houses constituted of representatives taken from British India as well as Indian States. I hope the Muslim delegates are fully aware of the implications of the federal scheme as discussed in the Round Table Conference. The question of Muslim representation in the proposed all-India federation has not yet been discussed. "The interim report," says Reuters' summary, "contemplates two chambers in the Federal Legislature, each containing representatives both of British India and States, the proportion of which will be a matter of subsequent consideration under the heads which have not yet been referred to the Sub-Committee." In my opinion the question of proportion is of the utmost importance and ought to have been considered simultaneously with the main question of the structure of the Assembly.

[[6d]] The best course, I think, would have been to start with a British Indian Federation only. A federal scheme born of an unholy union between democracy and despotism cannot but keep British India in the same vicious circle of a unitary Central Government. Such a unitary form may be of the greatest advantage to the British, to the majority community in British India, and to the Indian Princes; it can be of no advantage to the Muslims, unless they get majority rights in five out of eleven Indian provinces with full residuary powers, and one-third share of seats in the total House of the Federal Assembly. In so far as the attainment of sovereign powers by the British Indian provinces is concerned, the position of His Highness the Ruler of Bhopal, Sir Akbar Hydari, and Mr. Jinnah is unassailable. In view, however, of the participation of the Princes in the Indian Federation, we must now see our demand for representation in the British Indian Assembly in a new light. The questions is not one of [the] Muslim share in a British Indian Assembly, but one which relates to representation of British Indian Muslims in an All-India Federal Assembly. Our demand for 33 per cent must now be taken as a demand for the same proportion in the All-India Federal Assembly, exclusive of the share allotted to the Muslim states entering the Federation.

[[7]] The Problem of Defence

[[7a]] The other difficult problem which confronts the successful working of a federal system in India is the problem of India's defence. In their discussion of this problem the Royal Commissioners have marshalled all the deficiencies of India in order to make out a case for Imperial administration of the Army. "India and Britain," say the Commissioners, "are so related that India's defence cannot, now or in any future which is within sight, be regarded as a matter of purely Indian concern. The control and direction of such an army must rest in the hands of agents of Imperial Government." Now, does it [not] necessarily follow from this that further progress towards the realisation of responsible government in British India is barred until the work of defence can be adequately discharged without the help of British officers and British troops? As things are, there is a block on the line of constitutional advance. All hopes of evolution in the Central Government towards the ultimate goal prescribed in the declaration of 20th August 1917, are in danger of being indefinitely frustrated, if the attitude illustrated by the Nehru Report is maintained, that any future change involves the putting of the administration of the army under the authority of an elected Indian Legislature. Further to fortify their argument they emphasize the fact of competing religions and rival races of widely different capacity, and try to make the problem look insoluble by remarking that "the obvious fact that India is not, in the ordinary and natural sense, a single nation is nowhere made more plain than in considering the difference between the martial races of India and the rest." These features of the question have been emphasised in order to demonstrate that the

British are not only keeping India secure from foreign menace but are also the "neutral guardians" of internal security.

[[7b]] However, in federated India, as I understand federation, the problem will have only one aspect, i.e. external defence. Apart from provincial armies necessary for maintaining internal peace, the Indian Federal Congress can maintain, on the north-west frontier, a strong Indian Frontier Army, composed of units recruited from all provinces and officered by efficient and experienced military men taken from all communities. I know that India is not in possession of efficient military officers, and this fact is exploited by the Royal Commissioners in the interest of an argument for Imperial administration. On this point I cannot but quote another passage from the Report which, to my mind, furnishes the best argument against the position taken up by the Commissioners. "At the present moment," says the Report, "no Indian holding the King's Commission is of higher army rank than a captain. There are, we believe, 39 captains of whom 25 are in ordinary regimental employ. Some of them are of an age which would prevent their attaining much higher rank, even if they passed the necessary examination before retirement. Most of these have not been through Sandhurst, but got their Commissions during the Great War." Now, however genuine may be the desire, and however earnest the endeavour to work for this transformation, overriding conditions have been so forcibly expressed by the Skeen Committee (whose members, apart from the Chairman and the Army Secretary, were Indian gentlemen) in these words: Progress...must be contingent upon success being secured at each stage and upon military efficiency being maintained, though it must in any case render such development measured and slow. A higher command cannot be evolved at short notice out of existing cadres of Indian officers, all of junior rank and limited experience. Not until the slender trickle of suitable Indian recruits for the officer class – and we earnestly desire an increase in their numbers – flows in much greater volume, not until sufficient Indians have attained the experience and training requisite to provide all the officers for, at any rate, some Indian regiments, not until such units have stood the only test which can possibly determine their efficiency, and not until Indian officers have qualified by a successful army career for the high command, will it be possible to develop the policy of Indianisation to a point which will bring a completely Indianised army within sight. Even then years must elapse before the process could be completed."

[[7c]] Now I venture to ask: who is responsible for the present state of things? Is it due to some inherent incapacity of our martial races, or to the slowness of the process of military training? The military capacity of our martial races is undeniable. The process of military training may be slow as compared to other processes of human training. I am no military expert to judge this matter. But as a layman I feel that the argument, as stated, assumes the process to be practically endless. This means perpetual bondage for India, and makes it all the more necessary that the Frontier Army, as suggested by the Nehru Report, be entrusted to the charge of a committee of defence, the personnel of which may be settled by mutual understanding.

[[7d]] Again, it is significant that the Simon Report has given extraordinary importance to the question of India's land frontier, but has made only passing references to its naval position. India has doubtless had to face invasions from her land frontier; but it is obvious that her present masters took possession of her on account of her defenceless sea coast. A self-governing and free India will, in these days, have to take greater care of her sea coast than [of her] land frontiers.

[[7e]] I have no doubt that if a Federal Government is established, Muslim federal States will willingly agree, for purposes of India's defence, to the creation of neutral Indian military and naval forces. Such a neutral military force for the defence of India was a reality in the days of Mughal rule. Indeed in the time of Akbar the Indian frontier was, on the whole, defended by armies officered by Hindu generals. I am perfectly sure that the scheme for a neutral Indian army, based on a federated India, will intensify Muslim patriotic feeling, and finally set at rest the suspicion, if any, of Indian Muslims joining Muslims from beyond the frontier in the event of an invasion.

[[8]] The Alternative

[[8a]] I have thus tried briefly to indicate the way in which the Muslims of India ought, in my opinion, to look at the two most important constitutional problems of India. A redistribution of British India, calculated to secure a permanent solution of the communal problem, is the main demand of the Muslims of India. If, however, the Muslim demand of a territorial solution of the communal problem is ignored, then I support, as emphatically as possible, the Muslim demands repeatedly urged by the All-India Muslim League and the All-India Muslim Conference. The Muslims of India cannot agree to any constitutional changes which affect their majority rights, to be secured by separate electorates in the Punjab and Bengal, or [which] fail to guarantee them 33 percent representation in any Central Legislature. There were two pitfalls into which Muslim political leaders fell. The first was the repudiated Lucknow Pact, which originated in a false view of Indian nationalism and deprived the Muslims of India of chances of acquiring any political power in India. The second is the narrow-visioned sacrifice of Islamic solidarity, in the interests of what may be called Punjab ruralism, resulting in a proposal which virtually reduces the Punjab Muslims to a position of minority. It is the duty of the League to condemn both the Pact and the proposal.

[[8b]] The Simon Report does great injustice to the Muslims in not recommending a statutory majority for the Punjab and Bengal. It would make the Muslims either stick to the Lucknow Pact or agree to a scheme of joint electorates. The despatch of the Government of India on the Simon Report admits that since the publication of that document the Muslim community has not expressed its willingness to accept any of the alternatives proposed by the Report. The despatch recognises that it may be a legitimate grievance to deprive the Muslims in the Punjab and Bengal of representation in the councils in proportion to their population merely because of weightage allowed to Muslim minorities elsewhere. But the despatch of the Government of India fails to correct the injustice of the Simon Report. In so far as the Punjab is concerned – and this is the most crucial point – it endorses the so-called "carefully balanced scheme" worked out by the official members of the Punjab Government which gives the Punjab Muslims a majority of two over Hindus and Sikhs combined, and a proportion of 49 percent of the House as a whole. It is obvious that the Punjab Muslims cannot be satisfied with less than a clear majority in the total House. However, Lord Irwin and his Government do recognise that the justification for communal electorates for majority communities would not cease unless and until by the extension of franchise their voting strength more correctly reflects their population; and further unless a two-thirds majority of the Muslim members in a provincial Council unanimously agree to surrender the right of separate representation. I cannot, however, understand why the Government of India, having recognised the legitimacy of the Muslim grievances, have not had the courage to recommend a statutory majority for the Muslims in the Punjab and Bengal.

[[8c]] Nor can the Muslims of India agree to any such changes which fail to create at least Sind as a separate province and treat the North-West Frontier Province as a province of inferior political status. I see no reason why Sind should not be united with Baluchistan and turned into a separate province. It has nothing in common with Bombay Presidency. In point of life and civilization the Royal Commissioners find it more akin to Mesopotamia and Arabia than India. The Muslim geographer Mas'udi noticed this kinship long ago when he said: "Sind is a country nearer to the dominions of Islam." The first Omayyad ruler is reported to have said of Egypt: "Egypt has her back towards Africa and face towards Arabia." With necessary alterations the same remark describes the exact situation of Sind. She has her back towards India and face towards Central Asia. Considering further the nature of her agricultural problems which can invoke no sympathy from the Bombay Government, and her infinite commercial possibilities, dependent on the inevitable growth of Karachi into a second metropolis of India, it is unwise to keep her attached to a Presidency which, though friendly today, is likely to become a rival at no distant period. Financial difficulties, we are told, stand in the way of separation. I do not know of any definite authoritative pronouncement on the matter. But assuming there are any such difficulties, I see no reason why the Government of India should not give temporary financial help to a promising province in her struggle for independent progress.

[[8d]] As to the North-West Frontier Province, it is painful to note that the Royal Commissioners have practically denied that the people of this province have any right to reform. They fall far short of the Bray Committee, and the Council recommended by them is merely a screen to hide the autocracy of the Chief Commissioner. The inherent right of the Afghan to light a cigarette is curtailed merely because he happens to be living in a powder house. The Royal Commissioners' epigrammatic argument is pleasant enough, but far from convincing. Political reform is light, not fire; and to light every human being is entitled, whether he happens to live in a powder house or a coal mine. Brave, shrewd, and determined to suffer for his legitimate aspirations, the Afghan is sure to resent any attempt to deprive him of opportunities of full self-development. To keep such a people contented is in the best interest of both England and India. What has recently happened in that unfortunate province is the result of a step-motherly treatment shown to the people since the introduction of the principle of self-government in the rest of India. I only hope that British statesmanship will not obscure its view of the situation by hoodwinking itself into the belief that the present unrest in the province is due to any extraneous causes.

[[8e]] The recommendation for the introduction of a measure of reform in the North-West Frontier Province made in the Government of India's despatch is also unsatisfactory. No doubt, the despatch goes farther than the Simon Report in recommending a sort of representative Council and a semi-representative cabinet, but it fails to treat this important Muslim province on [an] equal footing with other Indian provinces. Indeed the Afghan is, by instinct, more fitted for democratic institutions than any other people in India.

[[9]] The Round Table Conference

[[9a]] I think I am now called upon to make a few observations on the Round Table Conference. Personally I do not feel optimistic as to the results of this Conference. It was hoped that away from the actual scene of communal strife and in a changed atmosphere, better counsels would prevail and a genuine settlement of the differences between the two major communities of India would bring India's freedom within sight. Actual events, however, tell a different tale. Indeed, the discussion of the communal question in London has demonstrated more clearly than ever the essential disparity between the two great cultural units of India. Yet the Prime Minister of England apparently refuses to see that the problem of India is international and not national. He is reported to have said that "his government would find it difficult to submit to Parliament proposals for the maintenance of separate electorates, since joint electorates were much more in accordance with British democratic sentiments." Obviously he does not see that the model of British democracy cannot be of any use in a land of many nations; and that a system of separate electorates is only a poor substitute for a territorial solution of the problem. Nor is the Minorities Sub-Committee likely to reach a satisfactory settlement. The whole question will have to go before the British Parliament; and we can only hope that the keen-sighted representatives of [the] British nation, unlike most of our Indian politicians, will be able to pierce through the surface of things and see clearly the true fundamentals of peace and security in a country like India. To base a constitution on the concept of a homogeneous India, or to apply to India principles dictated by British democratic sentiments, is unwittingly to prepare her for a civil war. As far as I can see, there will be no peace in the country until the various peoples that constitute India are given opportunities of free self-development on modern lines without abruptly breaking with their past.

[[9b]] I am glad to be able to say that our Muslim delegates fully realise the importance of a proper solution of what I call [the] Indian international problem. They are perfectly justified in pressing for a solution of the communal question before the question of responsibility in the Central Government is finally settled. No Muslim politician should be sensitive to the taunt embodied in that propaganda word – communalism – expressly devised to exploit what the Prime Minister calls British democratic sentiments, and to mislead England into assuming a state of things which does not really exist in India. Great interests are at stake. We are 70 millions, and far more homogeneous than any other people in India. Indeed the Muslims of India are the only Indian people who can fitly be described as a nation in the modern sense of the word. The Hindus, though ahead of us in almost all respects, have not yet been able to achieve the kind of homogeneity which is necessary for a nation, and which Islam has given you as a free gift. No doubt they are anxious to become a nation, but the process of becoming a nation is kind of travail, and in the case of Hindu India involves a complete overhauling of her social structure.

[[9c]] Nor should the Muslim leaders and politicians allow themselves to be carried away by the subtle but fallacious argument that Turkey and Persia and other Muslim countries are progressing on national, i.e. territorial, lines. The Muslims of India are differently situated. The countries of Islam outside India are practically wholly Muslim in population. The minorities there belong, in the language of the Quran, to the 'people of the Book'. There are no social barriers between Muslims and the 'people of the Book'. A Jew or a Christian or a Zoroastrian does not pollute the food of a Muslim by touching it, and the law of Islam allows intermarriage with the 'people of the Book'. Indeed the first practical step that Islam took towards the realisation of a final combination of humanity was to call upon peoples possessing practically the same ethical ideal to come forward and combind. The Quran declares: "O people of the Book! Come, let us join together on the 'word' (Unity of God), that is common to us all." The wars of Islam and Christianity, and later, European aggression in its various forms, could not allow the infinite meaning of this verse to work itself out in the world of Islam. Today it is being gradually realised in the countries of Islam in the shape of what is called Muslim Nationalism.

[[9d]] It is hardly necessary for me to add that the sole test of the success of our delegates is the extent to which they are able to get the non-Muslim delegates of the Conference to agree to our demands as embodied in the Delhi Resolution. If these demands are not agreed to, then a question of a very great and far-reaching importance will arise for the community. Then will arrive the moment for independent and concerted political action by the Muslims of India. If you are at all serious about your ideals and aspirations, you must be ready for such an action. Our leading men have done a good deal of political thinking, and their thought has certainly made us, more or less, sensitive to the forces which are now shaping the destinies of peoples in India and outside India. But, I ask, has this thinking prepared us for the kind of action demanded by the situation which may arise in the near future?

[[9e]] Let me tell you frankly that, at the present moment, the Muslims of India are suffering from two evils. The first is the want of personalities. Sir Malcolm Hailey and Lord Irwin were perfectly correct in their diagnosis when they told the Aligarh University that the community had failed to produce leaders. By leaders I mean men who, by Divine gift or experience, possess a keen perception of the spirit and destiny of Islam, along with an equally keen perception of the trend of modern history. Such men are really the driving forces of a people, but they are God's gift and cannot be made to order.

[[9f]] The second evil from which the Muslims of India are suffering is that the community is fast losing what is called the herd instinct. This [loss] makes it possible for individuals and groups to start independent careers without contributing to the general thought and activity of the community. We are doing today in the domain of politics what we have been doing for centuries in the domain of religion. But sectional bickerings in religion do not do much harm to our solidarity. They at least indicate an interest in what makes the sole principle of our structure as a people. Moreover, the principle is so broadly conceived that it is almost impossible for a group to become rebellious to the extent of wholly detaching itself from the general body of Islam. But diversity in political action, at a moment when concerted action is needed in the best interests of the very life of our people, may prove fatal.

[[9g]] How shall we, then, remedy these two evils? The remedy of the first evil is not in our hands. As to the second evil, I think it is possible to discover a remedy. I have got definite views on the subject; but I think it is proper to postpone their expression till the apprehended situation actually arises. In case it does arise, leading Muslims of all shades of opinion will have to meet together, not to pass resolutions, but finally to determine the Muslim attitude and to show the path to tangible achievement. In this address I mention this alternative only because I wish that you may keep it in mind and give some serious thought to it in the meantime.

[[10]] The Conclusion

[[10a]] Gentlemen, I have finished. In conclusion I cannot but impress upon you that the present crisis in the history of India demands complete organisation and unity of will and purpose in the Muslim community, both in your own interest as a community, and in the interest of India as a whole. The political bondage of India has been and is a source of infinite misery to the whole of Asia. It has suppressed the spirit of the East and wholly deprived her of that joy of self-expression which once made her the creator of a great and glorious culture. We have a duty towards India where we are destined to live and die. We have a duty towards Asia, especially Muslim Asia. And since 70 millions of Muslims in a single country constitute a far more valuable asset to Islam than all the countries of Muslim Asia put together, we must look at the Indian problem not only from the Muslim point of view, but also from the standpoint of the Indian Muslim as such. Our duty towards Asia and India cannot be loyally performed without an organised will fixed on a definite purpose. In your own interest, as a political entity among other political entities of India, such an equipment is an absolute necessity.

[[10b]] Our disorganised condition has already confused political issues vital to the life of the community. I am not hopeless of an intercommunal understanding, but I cannot conceal from you the feeling that in the near future our community may be called upon to adopt an independent line of action to cope with the present crisis. And an independent line of political action, in such a crisis, is possible only to a determined people, possessing a will focalised by a single purpose. Is it possible for you to achieve the organic wholeness of a unified will? Yes, it is. Rise above sectional interests and private ambitions, and learn to determine the value of your individual and collective action, however directed on material ends, in the light of the ideal which you are supposed to represent. Pass from matter to spirit. Matter is diversity; spirit is light, life and unity.

[[10c]] One lesson I have learnt from the history of Muslims. At critical moments in their history it is Islam that has saved Muslims and not vice versa. If today you focus your vision on Islam and seek inspiration from the ever-vitalising idea embodied in it, you will be only reassembling your scattered forces, regaining your lost integrity, and thereby saving yourself from total destruction. One of the profoundest verses in the Holy Quran teaches us that the birth and rebirth of the whole of humanity is like the birth and rebirth of a single individual. Why cannot you who, as a people, can well claim to be the first practical exponents of this superb conception of humanity, live and move and have your being as a single individual? I do not wish to mystify anybody when I say that things in India are not what they appear to be. The meaning of this, however, will dawn upon you only when you have achieved a real collective ego to look at them. In the words of the Quran, "Hold fast to yourself; no one who erreth can hurt you, provided you are well guided" (5:104).

Source: Speeches, Writings, and Statements of Iqbal, compiled and edited by Latif Ahmed Sherwani (Lahore: Iqbal Academy, 1977 [1944], 2nd ed., revised and enlarged), pp. 3-26.

www.ingramcontent.com/pod-product-compliance
Lightning Source LLC
Chambersburg PA
CBHW070209290526
45789CB00002B/949